Mind Is Neutrino!?

It Gives Evolution and Psychic Power

Hideo Asawa

Contents

Preface

The content of this book is the result of a philosophical approach to the unified theory of the universe. Simply put, both the matter of the universe and mind of living things are derived from the fundamental ultrafine things. In other words, mind is real existence like an elementary particle. So, both modern science and religion need to rethink the workings of mind.

In my view, philosophy established by Dr. Kenzo Yamamoto - namely a 6-dimensional principle - represents the truth of the universe. I will briefly explain the 6-dimensional principle in this book. To prove that it is really the truth of the universe, I have thought that it would be good if the fundamentals of cosmophysics could be explained in the 6-dimensional principle.

To describe the conclusion first, considering that the universe is 6-dimensional according to the 6-dimensional theory, the root of the universe can be explained by the "Proto-particle" (Philosophical tetrahedron) that I named. And the elementary particles that make up substances can be explained in a unified way as phenomena of "Proto-particles".

For more information on this cosmology, please read next my book.

True Identity of Dark Matter!? "Proto-Particle" Produce Elementary Particles

By the way, it was end of 2014 when I came up with the "Proto-particle" (philosophical tetrahedron). I published it on the homepage in the spring of 2015, but it was difficult to understand, so I revised it in various ways and it became this book.

Experience of the power of mind

The characteristic of the 6-dimensional principle is to recognize not only material but also the existence of mind and its power.

Most of thc so-callcd materialists, who think that modern science is absolutely and mind is a phenomenon that occurs in the physical and electrical functions of brain cells, do not admit that there is power in mind. However, it is not idealism that believes in the occult or the power of God.

I hope scientists do not deny new possibilities that like as cannot be explained by conventional science but can be explained by the theory of relativity. It is after all not so rare for people to experience something they cannot explain but refer to as "foreboding" or "sixth sense".

I used to think that materialism was correct, but when I was young, I had a mystical experience and changed my idea.

When I was a college student, I went far away with my fellow students by senior's car. I drove happily on the way. However, when we were about to return, I suddenly felt something like chills and said, "I don't want to drive," but I couldn't resist my senior and drove again. But I couldn't go against my senior and I drove again. As a result, we had an accident that our car was hit by a taxi on the way. No one was injured, but I was shocked at the first experience.

I wondered if I had predicted it with a sixth sense.

Also, I repeated the following experiment several times. I close my eyes, think hard of a certain card and send it to my friend telepathically. My friend is able to choose the same card from a bunch of cards. Most of these experiments were successful.

I didn't do any more, but I was convinced that telepathy really existed.

At a concentration game, I was able to guess correctly several cards that have not been opened even once when in good condition. However, the cards were not clearly visible in my mind’s eye, then it was intuition.

Unfortunately, I haven't trained since then, so these abilities seem to have diminished.

The most important experience is about infertility treatment for me and my wife. When I do mental unification every day and thought hard that the treatment would be successful, the result was a little better, but when I didn't do it, the result was bad. So, I was able to recognize the power of own mind.

It seems that if you think hard about it with mental unification, you can influence living things even if you do not have the power to move things. When your child or pet is sick, it will work a little if you think hard about their recovery, so it is a good idea to give it a try.

This mental unification is an ancient Japanese method, and Dr. Kenzo Yamamoto was spreading it. This is also called psychokinesis.

Including as a judgment material these my real experiences of feeling the power of own mind, I think that the 6-dimensional principle that recognizes the reality of mind and its power is correct.

If the 6-dimensional principle is the truth of the universe, it should also be applicable to life and mind that were born in the universe.

1. The universe is six-dimensional

1-1. Philosophy of the 6-dimensional principle

According to the 6-dimensional principle, the philosophical theory insisted by Dr. Kenzo Yamamoto (Nov. 12, 1912-Aug. 7, 2007), there are 4 elements in human perception and world events and phenomena: space, time, power (energy) and intention (direction).

Space has 3 dimensions: height, width and depth, while time, power and intention each has 1 dimension. So, there are 6 dimensions in the 4 elements. Hence it is called 6-dimensional principle.

This can be visualized as shown in the figure below.

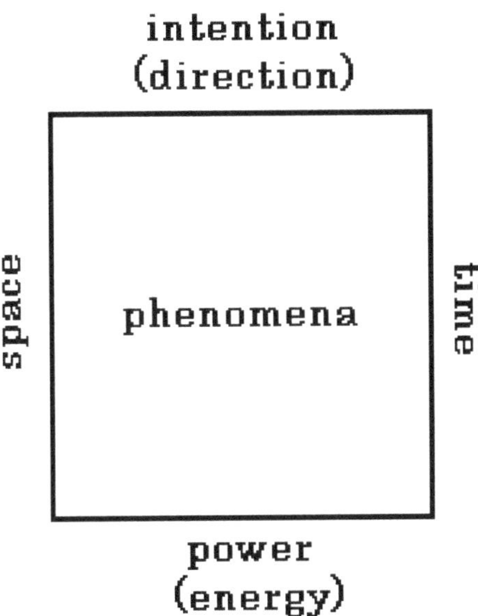

Ideally, people shouldn't be biased towards any of these 4 elements, but unfortunately most people's ideas are biased towards any.

In the world, a culture of thinking with easy-to-understand antinomy such as winning and losing, good and evil, pros and cons, yin and yang, high and low, 1 or 0, etc. has developed, but there are actually 4.

As a simple example, we often divide the world into west and east, but we need 4 in reality, including north and south.

Furthermore, when applying this 6-dimensional principle to human thought, for example, if you are biased towards space or power, you will be hedonism (such as good if happy now) or materialism (such as money or power is all).

Conversely, if you are biased towards time or intention, you will be fundamentalism (such as absolute habits) or spiritualism (such as superstitious religion).

And, when biased like these, people make mistakes in their lives by fighting for money or religion, or ignoring medicine and being too late.

So, the center, having no biases toward either, is our ideal position.

Changing the representation in the above figure, it will be as shown in the following figure.

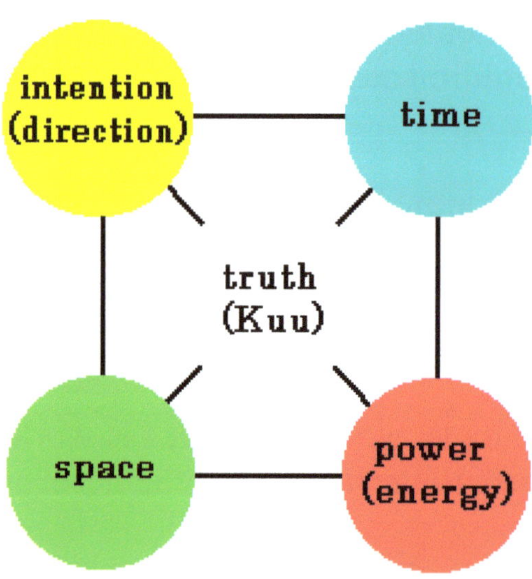

The truth is in the center, not biased toward any element. The middle "Kuu" will be explained in Chapter 3.

1-2. Why is it 6-dimensional rather than 4-dimensional?

Einstein concluded that the universe has 4 dimensions, consisting of space (3-dimensional) and time. Why is it need 2 more dimensions, power and intention?

Dr. Yamamoto discovered it while working in a rice field, so I will explain it in that situation.

If in the 4-dimensional world, you want to work with a hoe in a rice field, but you keep standing like a scarecrow in that space and only time passes, and you cannot do anything. In order for you to work with a hoe, you need the power to move the tool and the will to move it. Dr. Yamamoto considers this power and will (intention) as 2 different dimensions.

He concluded that the universe is 6 dimensions, which is 4 dimensions (space and time) plus that 2 dimensions (power and intention), and that it is the minimum number of dimensions required.

1-3. Power should be the 5th dimension

It is strange that power is not considered as a dimension in physics.

Regarding the motion of an object, the physics formula is:

<Force> = <Mass> x <Acceleration>

Acceleration is a value determined by the 4 dimensions of position (space) and time.

Then, how about mass?

After all, if we do not know acceleration or gravity and force or energy, we cannot determine mass.

Dimension is the minimum required measure to represent an event. Namely, I think it is necessary to regard force or energy as the 5th dimension.

On the other hand, in physics, there is a theory that the universe is 5-dimensional. And, as an explanation of the 5th dimension, it is said that there is a parallel universe, but isn't it more realistic to think of power as the 5th dimension, rather than fantasizing about a parallel universe?

1-4. Intention (direction) is also a dimension of the universe

As Dr. Yamamoto thought, intention (direction) is important in expressing the events of the world.

No event will occur unless you determine what and how, or in which direction. In mathematics, we think of a vector (direction with size), but it is not treated as a dimension. However, intention (direction) is also the minimum necessary physical scale to represent an event.

In other words, I think we need to think about the intention or direction as the 6th new dimension.

I think that mind is an accumulation of intention, but general physicists will not admit intention as a dimension. Scientists typically regard mind as a temporary state of physical or electrical action of brain cells and believe that it is impossible to act on matter in reverse.

In recent years, it has been said that it is natural for mind to affect the body, but the process is considered only as a material mechanism by which chemical substances are secreted by signals from brain cells.

According to research by Dr. Yamamoto, in the 6-dimensional world, a material phenomenon without being limited by space and time is happened by the effect of intention, and that phenomenon can exceed the speed of light. Then, it will be possible that mysterious quantum entanglement or quantum teleportation which instantly transmits information between elementary particles far apart at the universe level.

I define to this ability of intention as "long-distance instantaneous communication capability between elements of intention," as described after.

I think that we can contribute to the development of physics by studying the action on matter with the intention as the 6th dimension.

2. The root body of the universe (Proto-particle) is a philosophical tetrahedron

2-1. Changing the expression becomes a philosophical tetrahedron

The figure below is a planar representation of the 6-dimensional principle described in 1-1.

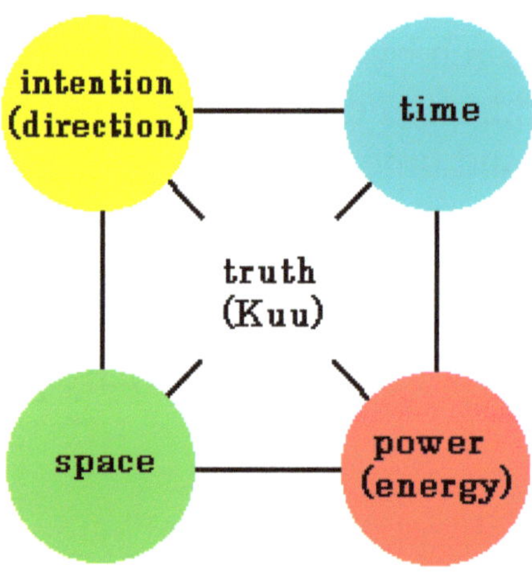

Changing it to a 3-dimensional expression will result in a tetrahedron (triangular pyramid) as shown below.

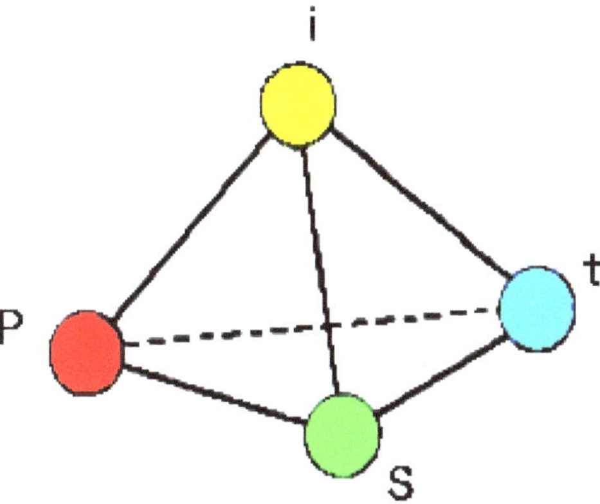

Here I express space as s, time as t, power as p, and intention as i. 4 colors are used for identification, they have no meaning in themselves.

Since this is a structure considered in terms of philosophical theory, I will call it a (6-dimensional) philosophical tetrahedron.

The following is the story of elementary particles, but it is necessary as a preliminary step to explain in Chapter 4 that a "mind element" is similar to neutrino.

2-2. Phenomenon faces of a philosophical tetrahedron

According to the 6-dimensional principle, since any event and phenomenon in the world (universe) is a complex of 4 elements, in the following figure of a philosophical tetrahedron, A, B, C and D is each considered as a phenomenon surface in which elements are biased (not all 4).

So, the elementary particles that make up the matter in the universe be able to consider to be phenomena on each side face.

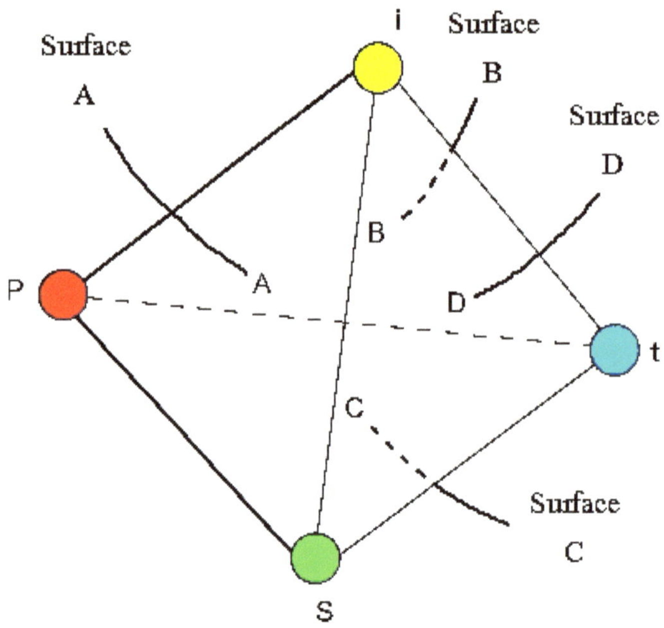

The relationship between each face of a philosophical tetrahedron and elementary particles is described in the following.

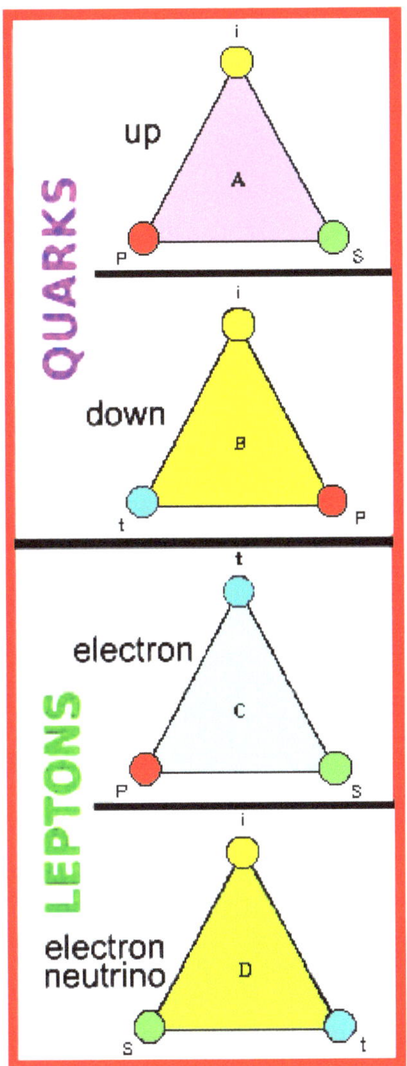

If the figure is changed into a 3-dimensional expression, it will look like this:

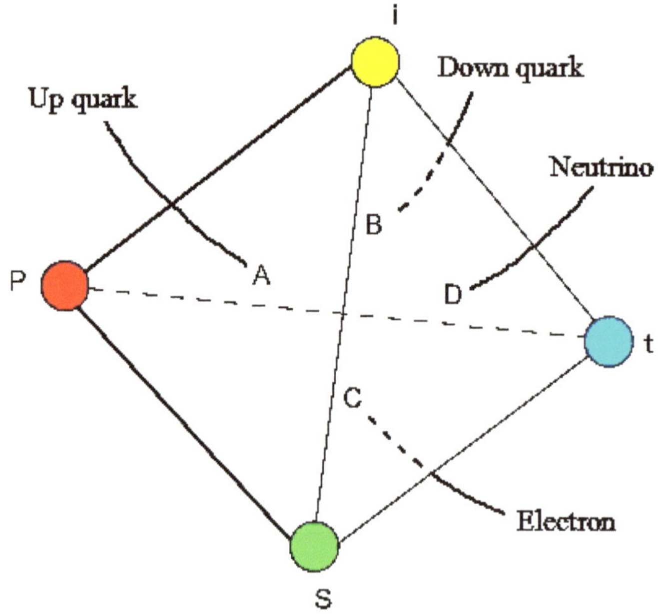

2-3. Elements of a philosophical tetrahedron, and elementary particles

In the figure above, the relationship between each phenomenon surface and the elementary particles is not randomly arranged by me. It takes into consideration the characteristics of each element (the vertex of the figure).

Regarding space, time, force, and intention of the 4 elements, I considered the dominant characteristics at the elementary particle level as follows:

* Space (s): Large, Wide

* Time (t): Long life

* Power (p): Strong force, Electromagnetic force, Large mass

* Intention (i): Instantaneous long-distance communication capability, Gravity, Memory

I will discuss gravity of the characteristic of the intention in the next section.

Considering these characteristics, in the case of quarks, since strong force acts, it contains p (power), and since it is affected by gravity, it also contains i (intention), so I place quarks as surface A and surface B.

Regarding electron, since strong force such as electromagnetic force acts, I place it as surface C, which contains p (power).

Since neutrino has a small mass and no electromagnetic force, I place it as surface D, which does not contain p (power).

By the way, what happens to the element that are not included in each phenomenon plane?

As mentioned earlier, the 4 elements -- space, time, power and intention -- cannot be separated. Therefore, since it is always a philosophical tetrahedron, element not included in the phenomenon plane is also connected and should exert some influence.

2-4. Intention elements produce gravity

If the intention element (i) (refer figure below) in the philosophical tetrahedron (Proto-particle) also has a memory, it should have the memory like a sense of unity that it was in a state of a single point just before the Big Bang at the beginning of the universe.

And due to that memory, all the philosophical tetrahedra (Proto-particle) that make up the present universe call each other by their communication capability such as quantum entanglement, and try to become one again.

I think this action produces the mutually attractive force, that is, gravity.

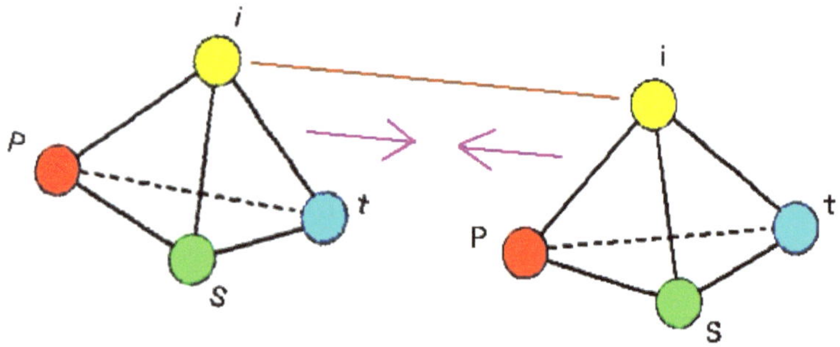

The idea that the element of intention creates gravity was first thought by Dr. Kenzo Yamamoto in his book "6-Dimensional Dialectic Method", but it was more conceptual.

3. "Kuu-ification" of a philosophical tetrahedron

3-1. State where phenomenon does not occur "Kuu"

According to the 6-dimensional principle of Dr. Yamamoto, if the 4 fundamental elements of this world and the universe - space, time, power and intention - melt into one, it becomes a state called "Kuu".

Dr. Yamamoto described that they melt into one, but it means the state that there is no bias in any of the four elements.

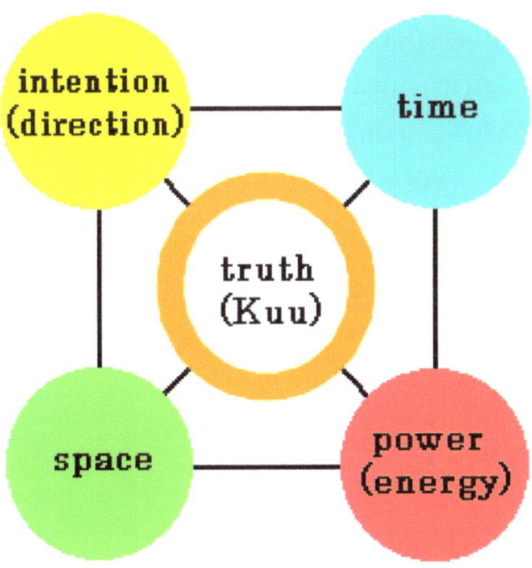

This word "Kuu" usually means empty, but here it's just a state that doesn't appear as a material phenomenon, and it is not completely nothingness.

In the 6-dimensional world, that is, in the universe, the state of "Kuu" and material phenomenon can occur reversibly.

Therefore, paranormal phenomena such as substances appearing or disappearing suddenly, which cannot be explained by conventional physics, can occur.

Dr. Yamamoto actually experienced many such phenomena and he called them collectively "Kuu-ification" (emptying) phenomenon.

[Column] -- Buddhist Kuu --

By the way, according to Dr. Yamamoto, when a material phenomenon is expressed as "*Shiki* (color)", the above reversible phenomenon corresponds to the Buddhist teaching of "*Shiki soku ze Kuu, Kuu soku ze Shiki*". This sentence means "phenomenon (color) is Kuu, and Kuu is phenomenon".

3-2. The world of "Kuu"

Well, the philosophical tetrahedron (Proto-particle) in this "Kuu" state does not disappear, but is state that none of the four faces has become a phenomenon.

It is thought that a phenomenon occurs when the 4 elements are biased for some reason, and therefore the philosophical tetrahedron (Proto-particle) is materialized into an elementary particle.

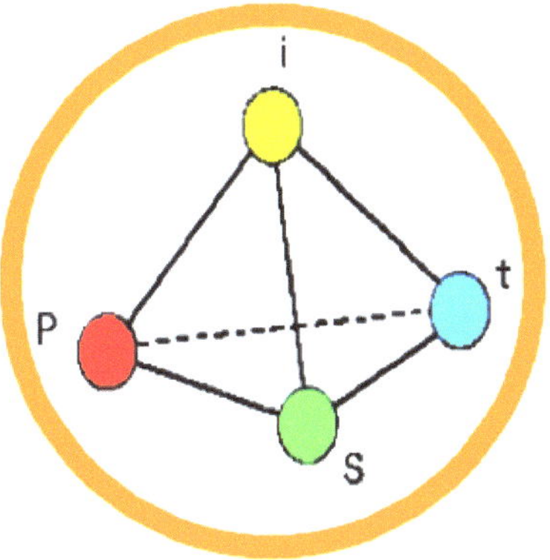

The philosophical tetrahedra (Proto-particles) in the state of "Kuu" do not emit material energy as if there is nothing, so they do not react with others and the size cannot be observed.

However, only intention elements will keep the ability to communicate with others, otherwise the above-mentioned reversible "Kuu-ification" (emptying) phenomenon cannot occur. Also, if the intention element with memory is not working even in a state of "Kuu", once the object has been "Kuu-ification" (emptying), it will never be able to return to the former, and its reappearance will not occur.

And this philosophical tetrahedron (Proto-particle) in the state of "Kuu" which is not materialized, has no reactivity, and has no size, may have been filled in the space around us and in the vacuum of the universe, like Dark matter.

4. A Mind element is a neutrino-like quantum

4-1. Mind element

In general, consciousness is the work of mind, and the soul is mind with individuality, but roughly speaking, both are mind. I will call the fundamental thing of the mind a "mind element". However, do not confuse it with the intention element.

According to philosopher Bergson, consciousness derives from memory. In other words, "the mind element is memory".

However, we cannot act if consciousness is only memory. Because, based on memory, we need to decide in which direction we should go. In other words, "the mind element is intention".

If both are correct, it means that "the mind element is memory and intention", and memory and intention are one. In other words, the intention element should have memory.

Brain scientists think that mind is derived from the electrical interaction of the cranial nerves network, that is, from electrical circuits like a computer.

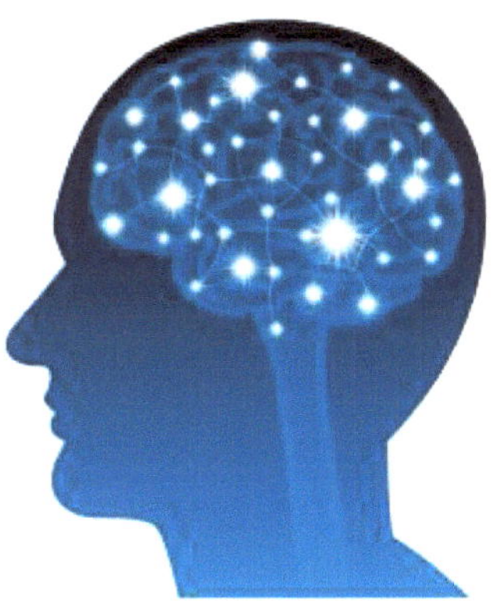

Image of cranial nerves network (Illust AC No1011157)

However, although computers can memorize, they have no free judgment ability like a human being has. Regardless of how advanced the deep learning function, etc. in computer gets, the function is in essence only to judge according to the conditions given by the programmer.

So, the intention is a position that uses memory. Therefore, the intention element is important to the creation of mind. And in the human body, it must be the philosophical tetrahedron that has the intention element.

From these, it is thought that many philosophical tetrahedra in the body are connected like a network by the communication ability of intention elements, and while retaining memory, they cooperate and play a central role such as judgment especially in the brain.

In that way, I think that one person's unique mind is formed.

Since philosophical tetrahedra including intention elements, which are the mind elements, are also the roots of substances, it is natural that mind and the body influence each other.

I think that since our body is active with mind, the mind works in cooperation with the brain made of substance, and due to the influence of the mind, electrons, one aspect of the philosophical tetrahedron, are used in the cranial nerves as electrical signals.

Then, it is no wonder that works like a computer or quantum computer are observed in the brain as the mind.

4-2. The mind element is the philosophical tetrahedron

Dr. Kenzo Yamamoto concluded that "the real body of the universe is a six-dimensional body". And he hypothesized that there are intention quarks as the mind elements apart from material quarks, and they have been in existence from the beginning of the universe when the Big Bang occurred.

On the other hand, he insisted that the four elements of space, time, power, and intention were inseparable and that the truth was that they were fused together.

I think that if the 6-dimensional principle is the fundamental truth of the universe, it should not be separate 6-dimensional bodies, the element of matter (quark) and the mind element (intention quark), but a unitary 6-dimensional body as the root body (Proto-particle) of the universe. That is the philosophical tetrahedron.

So, the mind element is considered the philosophical tetrahedron.

4-3. The mind element resembles a neutrino

What happens to mind (generally called a soul) of a person whose body has ceased to be? Even if the body is dead and decomposed to molecular level or atomic level, it is still a substance.

So far, ghosts have been confirmed all over the world, albeit in small numbers, but thcy act and talk, that is, they have mind. If mind arises from the brain's electrical circuit, there should be no mind after death as the brain no longer exists.

If we recognize the existence of mind (soul) after death, it means that mind (soul) can exist separately from the substances that constitute the body, including the brain.

A person should have many philosophical tetrahedra that are the elements of the mind. Since the soul after death is still working (thinking), that philosophical tetrahedron as the mind element seems to be a phenomenon rather than "Kuu-ification" (emptying) state.

Now consider the phenomenon faces of the philosophical tetrahedron. It is not a phenomenon face with power (p) such as substance that constitute the body. It is possibly face D which is composed of elements of s (space), t (time) and i (intention), without p (power). Elementary particle as a phenomenon on face D is neutrino. So, I think the mind element is similar to neutrino.

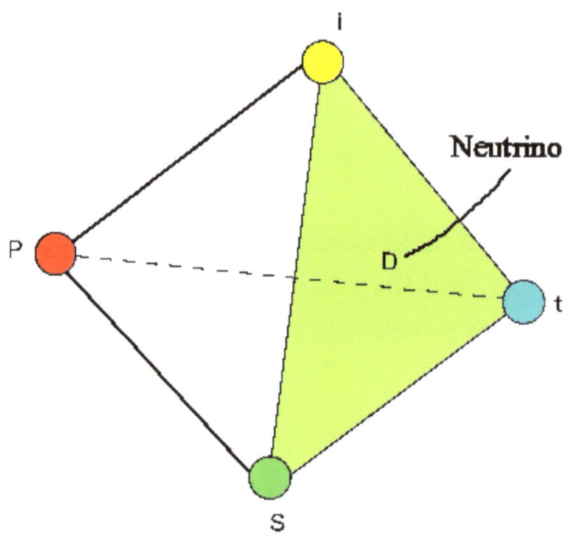

If you concentrate your mind and send psychokinesis to a device that responds to neutrinos, you may get a significant result.

4-4. Characteristic of the mind element

Since neutrinos are generated by the nuclear fusion reaction of stars, etc., they are usually flying at high speeds in space.

Compared to that, the elements of the mind that resemble neutrinos are static. Other than that, like neutrinos, it should be easy to get through objects. And although it is affected by gravity, it is very small.

On the other hand, intention elements (i) of many mind elements (philosophical tetrahedra) in the body have memories, and further form an aggregate of the mind elements by mutual communication ability, and even without substances as a body they can constitute a personality with an individuality called a soul, I think.

So, a human neutrino-like soul can pass through a wall. A ghost as a soul with ethereal body, can also pass through walls. And a neutrino-like soul can also telepathize with a person far away.

Since ghosts often appear in the form of the whole body, I think that the mind elements (philosophical tetrahedra) will exist throughout the body and keep their memory. That means, there should be a part of the soul in the part of the body.

Therefore, in transplantation surgery, I think it may happen that the personality (soul) of a person who has transplanted an organ which has the mind elements of another person is affected and changes slightly after the transplantation.

4-5. Verify the weight of the soul with neutrinos

One study shows that when a person dies, he loses about 20 grams, which is the weight of his soul. That was announced in 1907 by an American doctor Duncan MacDougall based on his experiment. The accuracy of the experiment seems doubtful, but I am referring to it.

There are variations in the results of the experiment, and especially in the case of dogs, it seems that there was almost no decrease. As one of the factors that make this experiment difficult, the premise that the soul will leave the body immediately after death is not certain. Different people have different ideas about after death. For example, in the case like a dog which not consider about after death, there is a possibility that the soul does not leave the body after death.

As mentioned earlier, since the mind elements are similar to neutrinos, I calculated the weight of the soul, which is the aggregate of the mind elements, using the mass of the neutrino, and examine whether it is around 20 grams.

First, let's show only my calculation results.

There are 3 types (generations) of neutrinos, so there are three results.

* In the case of electron neutrino: Soul weight < 0.00027 g

* In the case of muon neutrino: Soul weight < 18 g

* In the case of tauon neutrino: Soul weight < 1800 g

From above results, if it is true that the soul weight is about 20 grams, it is possible that the mind element is muon neutrino.

The possibility of it being electron neutrino cannot be ruled out either, but tauon neutrino appears to be too heavy.

However, in the calculation process I assumed that "1 mind element exists in 1 atom of a human body", but there is no evidence for that hypothesis.

1 atom is composed of several or dozens of material elementary particles, but I thought that there will be at least 1 mind element like as a neutrino in each atom.

The individual cells that make up the human body are the smallest living organisms. Unicellular organisms, such as amoebas, behave as if they have will without a brain. From that, it is thought that there are many mind elements within one cell.

Since an atom make up the cell is made up of elementary particles, the mind element should be able to exist which is similar to an elementary particle.

-- Calculation process --

I assume that

* Because a ghost may appear as the whole body of a person after death, there are the mind elements in a whole body;

* There is 1 mind element in each 1 of the atoms of a human cell;

* All the mind elements in the human body gather and become a soul of the person.

Then, it will be

[Soul weight] = [Number of atoms in a human body] × [Weight of a neutrino]

* Number of atoms contained in one human cell: 1000 trillion (10^{15}).

* Number of cells contained in a human body: 60 trillion (6×10^{13}).

Then, from the above,

[Number of atoms in a human body] = 6×10^{28}

Also,

Convert a neutrino mass to weight with 1 MeV = 1.8×10^{-27} g,

* Mass of electron neutrino < 2.5 eV = about 4.5×10^{-3} g

* Mass of muon neutrino < 170 keV = about 3×10^{-28} g

* Mass of tauon neutrino < 18 MeV = about 3×10^{-26} g

I calculated the soul weight using the above numbers.

4-6. Mind elements in the brain

By the way, how many mind elements are there in the human brain?

Human's brain nerve cells are about 90 billion (9×10^{10} pieces). (Information of RIKEN)

Similar to the previous calculation process, if the number of atoms contained in 1 cell is 1000 trillion (10^{15}), and 1 atom has 1 mind element:

It will be, total number of mind elements of human brain nerve cells = about 9×10^{26} pieces.

Since the mind element has memory ability, let's think that 1 of them corresponds to 1 bit of computer memory.

Using familiar units, 8 bits = 1B (bytes), 1 trillion (10 ^ 12) = 1 tera, so the human brain corresponds to a supercomputer with 100 trillion times the memory of about 1TB (terabytes).

Moreover, since mind element is similar to a neutrino, it can be said to be a super quantum computer.

Considering this, the human brain seems to have great ability.

5. Mind produce evolution

5-1. Modern evolutionary theory is wrong

A combination of Darwin's theory of evolution that only life adapted to the environment survives, that is [natural selection + survival of the fittest], and Mendel's theory, that is [mutation + genetics], is currently the mainstream evolutionary theory called Neo-Darwinism.

But when it comes to mutations, humans usually get sick. Let's assume that a genetic abnormality causes a tumor in the human body. Does the tumor help a person adapt to the environment and live? The answer is no.

For example, a plant called Hammer Orchid (picture below) has such a mechanism:

Part of the flower resembles a female wasp in shape, color and scent, when a male wasp is attracted and jumps to it another part of the flower is bent, pollen is then attached to the back of the male wasp, which goes on to pollination.

Would such accidental mutations occur so conveniently and repeatedly in the Hammer Orchid?

No, the probability that such a coincidence occurs is infinitely close to zero, and it will not happen without planned genetic manipulation. Who on earth genetically engineered it? There can be no other but the Hammer Orchid itself.

(Quoted from https://kevinswildside.wordpress.com/tag/flora/)

There are many other examples of evolution where changes seem to have occurred as the flora and fauna had wanted. These cannot be explained with unplanned mutations. I can only think that evolution is influenced by the intention elements of the mind elements in the body of the flora and fauna.

I reckon that even without an eye or a nose, the Orchid is capable of perceiving the favorite appearance and smell of wasps by responding to the minds of wasps because it has intention elements. And I suppose that the mind in which the Orchid's intention elements gathered, including the genetic stage, affected the body, changing it as the Orchid wanted.

The story is a little off, I heard that when a person grows a plant by speaking to it or playing music, the plant grows well.

I think the intention of the mind of love for the plants of the people will respond to the intention of the plants.

(Illust AC No1378210)

5-2. Evolution as a desire of intention

According to Dr. Yamamoto, the universe has the intention of living toward the realization of value, but there is no such abstract concept in the intention element at the elementary particle level, and it should be much simpler than that.

I think, the extremely simple tendency of the intention element of the philosophical tetrahedron (Proto-particle) that fills the universe has gradually gained influence over time, it piles up and produces life, acquires the ability to live and eventually, only after becoming a human, it possesses the ability to think about philosophical concepts such as value.

Simply put, the extremely simple tendency of the intention elements gave rise to evolution.

Timeline of life evolution on earth

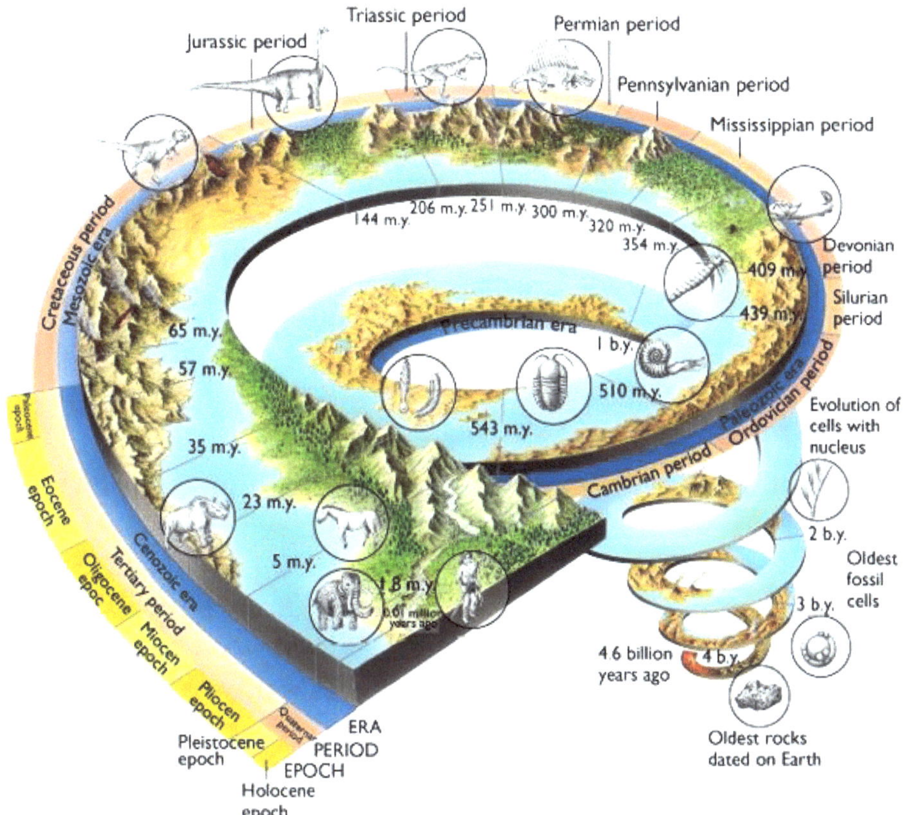

(https://academictips.org/blogs/timeline-of-life-evolution-on-earth/)

Then, what is the extremely simple tendency of the intention element that leads to evolution?

As mentioned in Chapter 2, it seems that:

the intention element of the philosophical tetrahedron that is the root body (Proto-particle) of the universe has memory like a sense of unity that it existed in the form of a single point before the universe was born at the Big Bang, and based on that memory, calling to return to the original even if it has scattered by the Big Bang creates gravity.

This tendency of the intention element can be said to be intention aiming for a unity where substances and mind are not separated.

Looking at the evolution from the position of intention aiming to unify substance and mind:

First, intention worked to make a life form from substances;

Then, it creates a brain where the intention can work intensively;

Eventually, it evolved into human with an advanced brain, and it became possible to take Nengraphy, etc.;

And, intention has acquired strong ability to act on substances.

Thinking that way, the evolution process seems to be in line with the aspiration of intention.

It can be said that "realization of value" is out of the question, but "the universe has intention to live" in that the trend of the intention elements of the philosophical tetrahedra omnipresent in the universe give rise to the evolution of life.

5-3. Humanity evolves into psychics?

If evolution is "the development of an ability of intention", although human beings are now stagnating their potential ability due to substance civilization, I believe eventually what is regarded as a supernatural power now could become a normal ability.

In other words, the ability of the intention to act on a substance becomes normal.

(Illust AC No940803)

Speaking of supernatural power, I do not mean the kind of "Superman" power that enables a person to fly in the sky or radiate heat rays from the eyes. I'm thinking of useful abilities such as avoiding danger by clairvoyance or intuition, communicating with family by telepathy about the danger, healing internal illnesses by concentration of mind, and so on.

According to Dr. Yamamoto, we cannot use supernatural power for bad purposes, so don't worry. And, he said everyone has the ability to improve the medical condition of the family by unifying mind, and it is "normal ability".

In that sense, human beings are already psychics.

It will make a leap, but if the supernatural power of human beings becomes even stronger, it may enable people to teleport objects such as UFOs to distant stars over space and time by combining the powers of many people.

6. Paranormal is possible by a philosophical tetrahedron

6-1. Nengraphy (Thoughtography)

When a person's consciousness (intention) is applied to a philosophical tetrahedron, the intention element of the philosophical tetrahedron reacts, and the power element is activated in the conscious place (space) and time. And it becomes possible to show material phenomena.

An optimal example of this is the Nengraphy (Thoughtography) that was discovered and studied in 1910 by Dr. Tomokichi Fukurai (Dec. 5, 1869-Mar. 13, 1952).

He carried out a large number of experiments and left a lot of Nengraphy taken by persons with this ability (hereafter referred to as "ability persons").

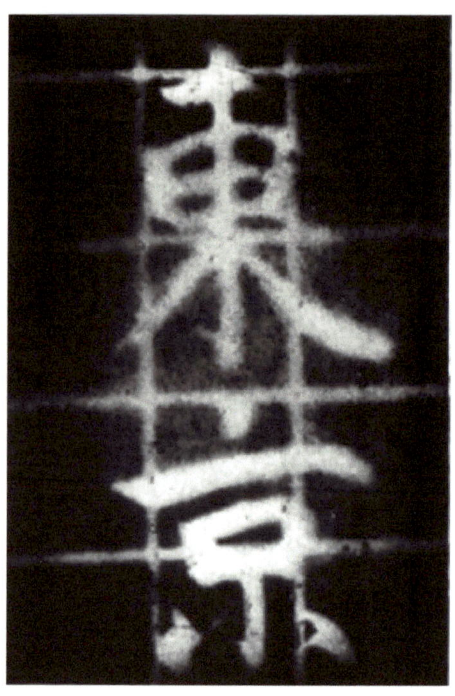

From Kenzo Yamamoto's "Nengraphy and Dr. Fukurai"

Nengraphy of character "Tokyo" by ability person, Ikuko Nagao

(Against the slander that she cuts out characters on thick paper placed on the photographic dry plate and expose the plate to radiation, she took the Nengraphy of the character with lines that would fall apart if cut.)

In the Nengraphy experiments, ability persons were able to take image of own mind to one or some, which specified by other person, of photographic dry plates (glass coated with photosensitizing agent) stacked in a pile.

This sensitization phenomenon of mind's power cannot be explained by conventional physics that does not recognize the intention elements.

Unfortunately, because it cannot be explained and the experiments cannot be reproduced unless there is an ability person, Nengraphy has been excluded from the study of physics and most scholars deny it.

However, if all things in the universe including humans are composed of philosophical tetrahedra, then it becomes possible to explain what is called wonders, such as ghosts, Nengraphy, clairvoyance, telepathy and "Kuu-ification" (emptying) phenomena that erases or presents substances.

6-2. Mechanism of Nengraphy

I will consider the mechanism of Nengraphy in a bit more detail.

In Nengraphy, the ability person concentrates the spirit and exposes characters and images on the photographic plate, but this exposure does not mean that the ability person emits energy such as electromagnetic waves or radiation. This is because even if several sheets of photographic plates are stacked in a pile, only one specific plate in them is exposed. If it is electromagnetic waves or radiation, other plates would also be exposed.

In ordinary photography, photosensitivity is caused by energy of light, which is electromagnetic wave, to act on photosensitizer to cause a chemical reaction, and an image is formed by changing the photosensitizer at that part. Even if it receives radiation instead of light, photosensitivity is caused by that energy. However, since Nengraphy does not depend on electromagnetic waves or radiation, chemical reactions should occur with different energy.

What is this other energy then? The energy that causes a chemical reaction should be material energy. However, if an ability person emits material energy, all photographic plates will be exposed, so it is incorrect. Then, energy is generated only in the desired part of the photosensitizer on the dry plate, and there is no choice but to cause a chemical reaction.

For example, as shown in the following figure,

If an ability person applies intensive thought to photograph a character "+" to Nengraphy:

By the communication capability of many intention elements (i) in the brain of the ability person,

A strong action occurs to the intention elements (i) of many philosophical tetrahedra at the part of "+" character of the photosensitizer on the photographic dry plate,

Each intention element (i) acts on the power element (p) of the same philosophical tetrahedron,

And, sufficient energy is generated in the part of "+" character for a chemical reaction to occur.

The above mechanism is conceivable.

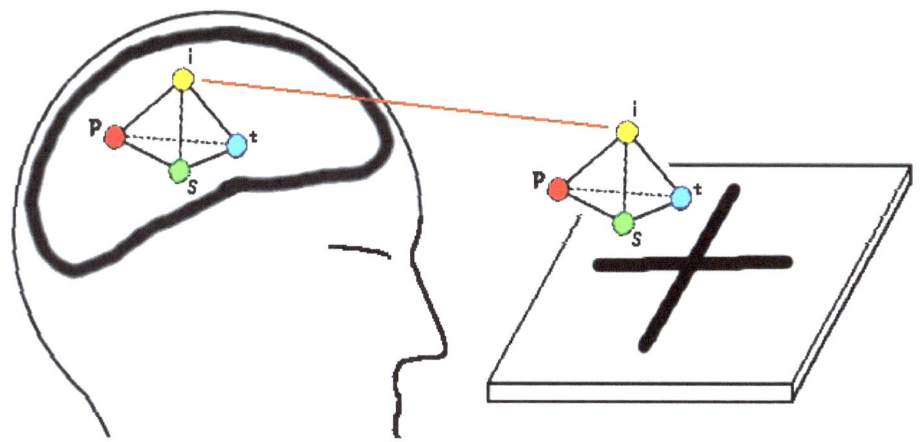

Apart from this method, it is also possible that the neutrino-like mind elements go out of the body by concentrating thinking and works directly on the intention elements (i) of philosophical tetrahedra of the photosensitizer.

I think that this mechanism of Nengraphy also applies to the mechanism of improving the illness by concentration of mind.

6-3. Mechanism of Teleportation

Let's consider a mechanism of "Kuu-ification" (emptying) phenomenon. "Kuu-ification" is as explained Chapter 3.

According to Dr. Yamamoto, "Kuu-ification" (emptying) phenomenon is an event in which substances and phenomena appear and disappear instantly, and he says that it will occur as a result of the ability person's concentrating consciousness.

Although elementary particle constituting a substance is in a phenomenon state of philosophical tetrahedron (Proto-particle), I think it can shift into a state of "Kuu" when the intention element act on other elements of own.

For example, as shown in the following figure,

If an ability person concentrates consciousness for erasing the sphere:

By the communication ability of many intention elements (i) in the brain of the ability person,

A strong approach occurs to the intention elements (i) of all the elementary particles (phenomenon state of philosophical tetrahedra) that constitute the sphere,

The intention element (i) acts on other elements of the same philosophical tetrahedron to become "Kuu" state,

And, the sphere is no longer a substance and disappears.

The above mechanism is conceivable.

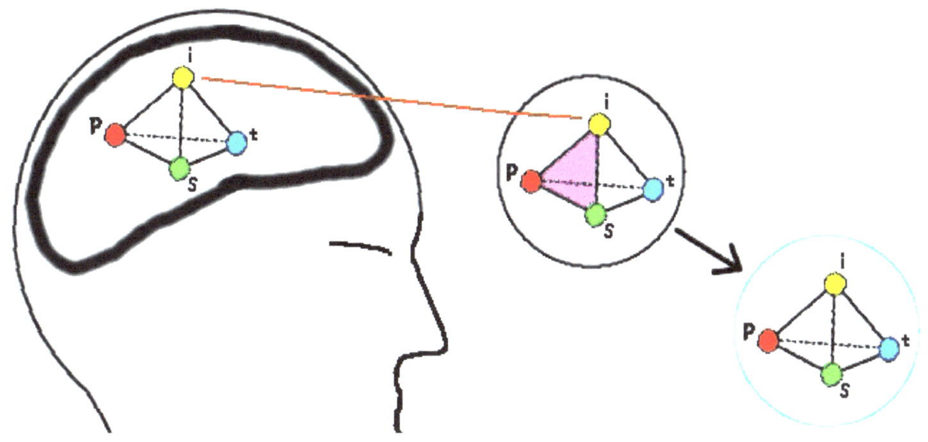

Also, apart from this method, a mechanism is also conceivable in which the neutrino-like element of the mind goes out of the body by concentrating thinking and works directly on the intention elements (i) of philosophical tetrahedra of the sphere.

Then, what happens to the sphere that disappeared?

For example, in the case of a gas, when it is put out in the air, it diffuses and disappears due to the influence of its own molecular motion, the air, etc.

However, since philosophical tetrahedra (Proto-particles) of the "Kuu-ification" (emptying) sphere are not substances, they should not be affected by such physical influences. But even in a state of "Kuu", the intention elements are working, and they have communication ability and memory ability.

Namely, the "Kuu-ification" (emptying) sphere does not diffuse and disappear, but it is considered to be in the state like one lump with the memory of the original shape (sphere). Therefore, if the ability person works to return to the original on the intention elements of the philosophical tetrahedra (Proto-particles) of the sphere which have been "Kuu-ification" (emptying) and disappeared, they return from the state of "Kuu" to the original phenomenon state as memorized, and the original sphere should appear.

Also, since an object in the state of "Kuu" should not be affected and bound by material influences of space, time and power, it can conceivably move far away instantly. That I consider to be the mechanism of Teleportation.

Contrary to erasing the sphere, when an ability person strongly tries to concentrate mind to emerge a sphere from an empty space, if the space is filled with philosophical tetrahedra (Proto-particles) (Dark matter?) in the state of "Kuu", it should be possible to make a sphere appear as a phenomenon from that space through working on intention elements of philosophical tetrahedra.

Afterword

In recent years, some scientists have used quantum random number generators to study how human consciousness acts on matter.

Dr. Dean Radin, a researcher in parapsychology from the Institute of Noetic Sciences, USA, observed that the unusual bias of several quantum random number generators occurred at the climax of burning a large doll in the Burning Man Festival which attracted 70,000 people.

Dr. Roger Nelson, a psychologist from Princeton University, USA, has been working on a research called "The Global Consciousness Project", whereby quantum random number generators are set at 50 locations in the world and kept under observation on a 24-hour basis. When the 9/11 terrorist attack in New York occurred in 2001, he observed anomalous bias of quantum random number generators in various parts of the world for several days.

These observations have accumulated data. However, the mechanism has not yet been elucidated.

As mentioned in this book, the element of the mind may be neutrinos. If so, the element of the mind behaves like a quantum, and it seems to be the mechanism by which mind affects matter.

Also, recently, hypothetical theory that quantum entanglement produces gravity appears to have been issued. This is similar to my opinion, "Gravity is occurred by the communication ability and their mutual call, of intention elements of the 'Proto-particles' (philosophical tetrahedra)".

I hope this book will be a clue to the elucidation of mind.

January 2022 Hideo Asawa

Matsumoto City, Nagano Prefecture, Japan
Graduated from Tokyo University of Science

For more information on Proto-particle and Dark matter, please read my book:

True Identity of Dark Matter!?

"Proto-Particle" Produce Elementary Particles.

Mind Is Neutrino!?

It Gives Evolution and Psychic Power

Published: March 2022

Author: Hideo Asawa

www.ingramcontent.com/pod-product-compliance
Ingram Content Group UK Ltd.
Pitfield, Milton Keynes, MK11 3LW, UK
UKHW060405300726
14090UKWH00006B/451

* 9 7 9 8 4 3 8 0 3 9 2 7 3 *